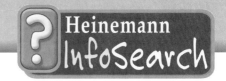

WHY DO I VOMIT?

✦ and other questions about digestion ✦

Angela Royston

Heinemann Library
Chicago, Illinois

Customer Service 888-454-2279
Visit our website at www.heinemannlibrary.com

Designed by Joanna Sapwell and StoryBooks
Illustrations by Nick Hawken
Originated by Ambassador Litho
Printed by South China Printers, Hong Kong

07 06 05 04 03
10 9 8 7 6 5 4 3 2 1

Library of Congress Cataloging-in-Publication Data
Royston, Angela.
  Why do I vomit? : and other questions about digestion / Angela
Royston.
      p. cm. -- (Body matters)
Includes index.
Summary: Answers common questions about the digestive system.
  ISBN 1-40340-206-X (HC)   ISBN 1-40340-461-5 (PB)
  1. Digestion--Juvenile literature. 2. Gastrointestinal
system--Juvenile literature. [1. Digestion. 2. Digestive system.] I.
Title. II. Series.
  QP145 .R693 2002
  612.3--dc21
                              2002003547

Acknowledgments
The author and publishers are grateful to the following for permission to reproduce copyright material:
pp. 4, 6, 9, 12, 15, 19, 20, 22, 24, 25, 26 Gareth Boden; pp. 11, 13, 17, 18 Science Photo Library; p. 21 FPG; p. 23 Popperfoto.

Cover photograph by Tudor Photography.

Some words are shown in bold, **like this.** You can find out what they mean by looking in the glossary.

CONTENTS

WHAT HAPPENS TO THE FOOD I EAT?

As this girl swallows a mouthful of her sandwich, the food begins a long journey through her body.

When you swallow a mouthful of food, it passes down a tube into your stomach. There it is churned around and broken up into smaller pieces. It then passes into your **intestines**—long tubes that join your stomach to your anus. On the way, the food is broken down into smaller and smaller pieces. Most of these very small pieces pass through the walls of the intestines into your blood. The rest is waste, and it leaves your body when you go to the bathroom.

Breaking up food

Food, such as cheese, bread, and fruit, contains the chemicals your body needs to survive and grow. But your body cannot use the chemicals as they exist in the cheese, bread, or tomato. Each food consists of several different chemicals, some of them combined together. The food has to be broken down into separate substances, or building blocks. This process is called digestion.

Digestion

The body has several ways of breaking down food. First, the teeth grind it up so that it mixes with saliva. Then the stomach mixes it around, like a food mixer. As it is being mixed, special chemicals called **enzymes** attack the particles of food and break them into separate building blocks. The building blocks then pass into the blood.

The digestive tube begins in the mouth and takes the food to the stomach. From there it passes through the small intestine. Waste food goes through the large intestine.

THE DIGESTIVE SYSTEM

The length of the digestive system from the mouth to the anus is more than five times as long as your total height. In an adult it is about 31 feet (9.5 meters) long.

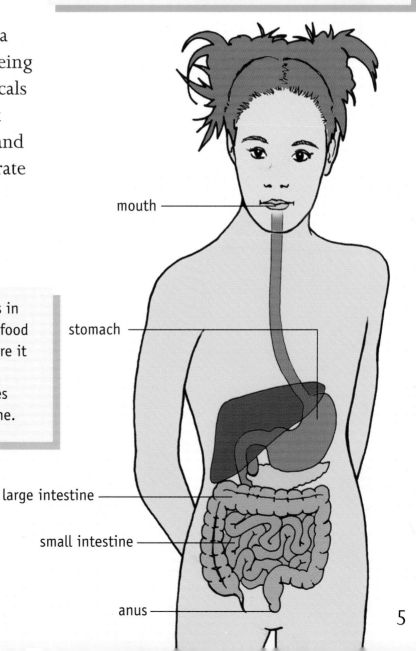

mouth

stomach

large intestine

small intestine

anus

5

WHY ARE TEETH DIFFERENT SHAPES?

You have two rows of teeth. The teeth in the upper jaw work against the teeth in the lower jaw to break up food—the first step in digestion.

Teeth are different shapes because they have different jobs to do. Your teeth work together to break food into smaller pieces. Each kind of tooth has a name. The flat, front teeth are called incisors. The pointed teeth behind them are the canines. The large, flat-topped teeth at the back of the mouth are molars.

A mouthful of teeth

Each tooth in your upper jaw is matched by the same kind of tooth in your lower jaw, and you have the same kinds of teeth on each side of your mouth. When a baby is born, its first set of teeth are already formed in the gums. As these teeth push through the gum, a second set, called permanent teeth, form below them. As a baby tooth falls out, it is replaced by a permanent tooth.

Incisors and canines

You have eight incisors, four in your upper jaw and four in your lower jaw. They are flat and sharp and slice through food like knives. You use them to bite into fruit and other solid food. Behind the incisors, you have four sharp, pointed canine teeth, one at each corner of the front of your mouth. They pierce food, such as meat, and grip it while you tear off a bite.

HARDER THAN BONE

Your teeth are coated with a layer of enamel, the hardest substance in the body. Below the enamel is dentine, which is as hard as bone.

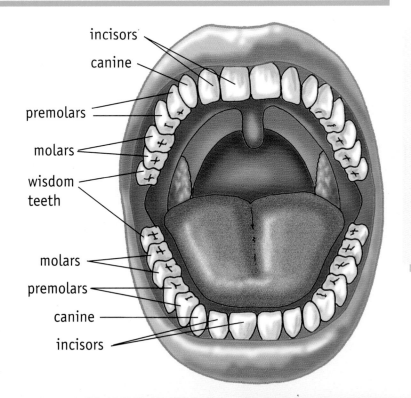

incisors
canine
premolars
molars
wisdom teeth
molars
premolars
canine
incisors

A complete set of permanent teeth. Baby teeth do not include all the back teeth, and the wisdom teeth only come through when you are about 18 years old or older.

Molars

Behind each canine tooth adults have are two flat-topped premolar teeth that grind up food. Behind the premolars are the molars. They are larger and bumpier than premolars, so they are even better at grinding up food.

Tongue and saliva

You cannot break down food with just your teeth. You need your tongue to push the food around your mouth. As you chew, saliva mixes with the food and makes it mushy and easy to swallow.

Swallowing

When the mouthful of food is mushy enough, the tongue pushes it to the back of your mouth. As soon as it touches the soft palate at the start of your throat, you automatically swallow. Special flaps close off the tubes to your nose and lungs so that you cannot breathe in air as you swallow.

The tongue takes the food to the back of the mouth and pushes it down the throat.

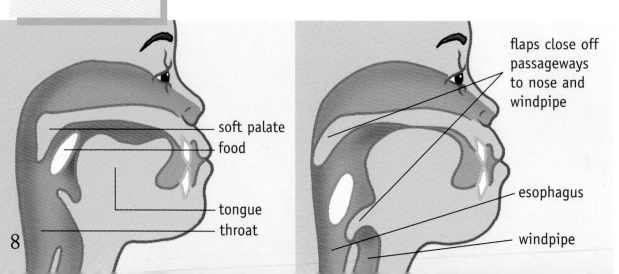

soft palate
food

flaps close off passageways to nose and windpipe

esophagus

tongue
throat

windpipe

Down the tube

The mouthful of food slides down the **esophagus** into your stomach. The walls of the esophagus close in behind the food and push it down, just like squeezing a tube of toothpaste. This means that you do not have to be upright to swallow food, but can swallow even when you are lying down. The walls of the esophagus are covered with **mucus** to help the food slide down.

This boy squeezes his candy out of the wrapper as he eats it. The food travels down his esophagus in a similar way.

CHOKING

Sometimes a crumb goes down the wrong tube. It goes into the windpipe, which leads to the lungs, instead of into the esophagus. Coughing usually pushes the crumb out.

HOW BIG IS MY STOMACH?

Your stomach stretches when you eat. A child's stomach can hold about 1 pint (.5 liter) of chewed up, mushy food. An adult's stomach holds about 2 pints (1 liter). This may not sound like very much, but food becomes less bulky when it is chewed up. Bread, for example, is mostly air.

Bands of stomach muscles move food in different directions.

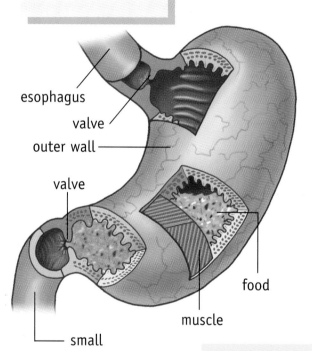

esophagus

valve

outer wall

valve

food

muscle

small intestine

Inside the stomach

The inner wall of the stomach is covered with many tiny pits. At the bottom of each pit is a **gland** that makes gastric juice—a strong acid that helps to kill any germs that you may have eaten with the food. It also helps to break down food. Between the outer and inner walls is a layer of strong muscles. They stir the food, squeeze it, and mash it into a slimy mush, called chyme.

FOOD IS MOSTLY WATER

vegetables:	about nine-tenths water
potatoes:	four-fifths water
rice:	about two-thirds water
chicken:	two-thirds water

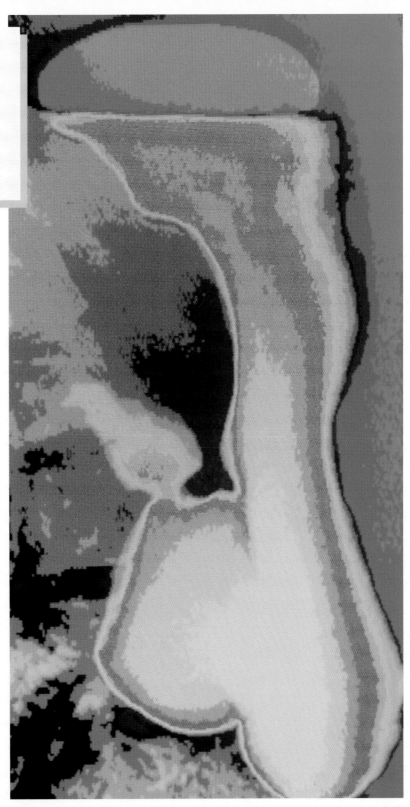

The stomach is shaped like a boxing glove. This is what the inside of your stomach looks like when it is empty.

Stomach valves

A **valve** is a device that allows something to move only in one direction. The valve at the top of the stomach stops food from moving from the stomach back up the **esophagus.** Food stays in the stomach until it has been mashed into chyme. A valve at the bottom of the stomach opens from time to time and a squirt of chyme passes into the small **intestine.**

WHY DO I VOMIT?

You vomit when your body needs to get rid of the contents of your stomach fast. Vomiting protects you from germs and poisons. The acidity in the **gastric** juices can kill many germs, but not all of them. If you have swallowed food that has too many germs for the gastric juices to kill, you will be sick. When some food goes bad, it produces poisons that may make you sick. The box opposite shows some of the things besides food poisoning that can make you vomit.

This boy has eaten some food that does not agree with him. He will feel better when he has vomited.

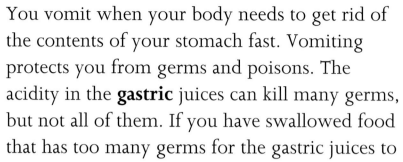

Forced out

When you vomit, the **diaphragm** pushes down on the stomach, forcing it to heave the unwanted food back up the **esophagus** and out through the mouth. The food is pushed the wrong way through the **valve** at the top of the stomach. Sometimes the valve relaxes by mistake, and a small amount of the contents of your stomach comes back up your esophagus. This gives you a burning feeling and a nasty taste in your mouth, but you are not actually sick.

Burping

Burping is when the valve at the top of the stomach opens to let gas out. Some foods produce more gas than others. Drinking carbonated drinks is likely to make you burp.

Rough water makes some people seasick. The movement of the boat disturbs the liquid in their ears and disturbs their sense of balance.

THINGS THAT CAN MAKE YOU SICK:

- bad smells, such as the smell of vomit
- illnesses such as scarlet fever or gastric flu
- migraine
- food allergy
- being anxious
- motion sickness, due to traveling in a car, bus, airplane, or boat
- rich food
- alcohol and other drugs

HOW LONG DOES FOOD STAY IN MY BODY?

Most food stays in your body for 16 to 24 hours. It takes about 5 seconds for a mouthful of food to slide down the **esophagus** to the stomach, but it will probably stay there for about 4 hours. The mushy food then passes a squirt at a time into the small **intestine.** The useful parts of the food are slowly digested. It takes about 5 hours for the rest of the food to pass right through the small intestine to the large intestine. Its progress slows down here, and it may be 7 to 16 hours later before undigested food finally leaves the body. Some food can take even longer.

The small intestine gets digestive juices from organs such as the gall bladder. Digested food passes from the small intestine into the blood.

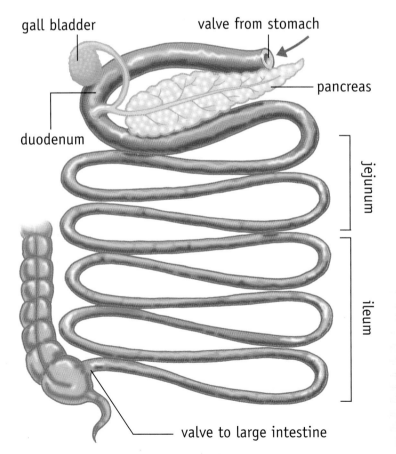

gall bladder

valve from stomach

pancreas

duodenum

jejunum

ileum

valve to large intestine

The small intestine

The small intestine consists of three parts—the duodenum, the jejunum, and the ileum. The duodenum is as long as twelve widths of your fingers. In adults this is about 10 inches (25 centimeters). Food stays in the duodenum for about an hour. While it is there it is mixed with digestive juices from the walls of the intestines and from the pancreas and gall bladder.

Bile works like dish soap. It breaks up fat into tiny droplets.

Digestive juices

Tubes from the pancreas and gall bladder feed into the duodenum and spray the chyme with digestive juices. The juice from the pancreas mixes with the chyme and neutralizes the strong acids made by the stomach. The gall bladder stores a bright green liquid, called bile, that is made by the liver. Bile breaks up fat into smaller drops that are easier for the body to digest.

Enzymes

Digestive juices contain several different **enzymes.** Enzymes are special chemicals that attach themselves to large, complicated **molecules** and break them up into smaller, simpler molecules that can be digested. The enzyme itself is not digested. After it has broken up one large molecule it floats away and attaches itself to another large molecule.

The villi

The villi are filled with tiny blood vessels. Simple food molecules pass through the walls of the villi into the blood.

The wall of the small **intestine** is lined with millions of villi. They look like tiny fingers sticking out from the wall of the intestine. Together they give the inner wall of the intestine a huge area for food to pass through. They are less than an inch long and are packed close together, like the bristles of a brush. Their walls are so thin that simple molecules pass through them into the blood. The blood, now rich with food molecules, is taken straight to the liver.

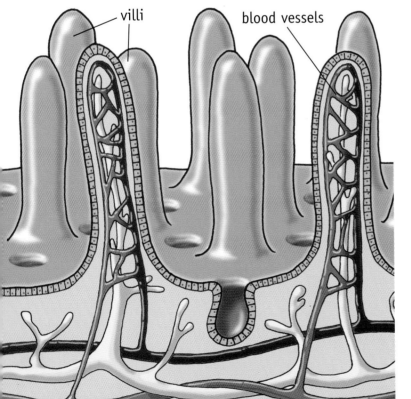

villi

blood vessels

The liver

The liver is the largest and one of the most important organs in the body. It takes food from the blood and stores some of it until it is needed. Then it releases the food into the blood.

OTHER THINGS THE LIVER DOES:
- filters waste and poisons out of the blood
- changes poisons into harmless substances
- sends poisons and waste to the kidneys
- produces a substance that helps blood to clot
- destroys dead red blood **cells**
- produces bile

This person is suffering from jaundice, an illness of the liver. The skin looks yellow because there is too much bile in the blood.

WHAT HAPPENS TO UNDIGESTED FOOD?

The large intestine is about 6 ½ feet (2 meters) long. It makes a large loop around the coils of the small intestine.

Undigested food passes from the small **intestine** through a **valve** into the large intestine. As it passes through the large intestine, water and **vitamins** and **minerals** are absorbed into the blood and the mushy paste slowly turns into soft solids, called **feces.** Feces are stored in the rectum, at the end of the large intestine, and leave the body when you go to the bathroom.

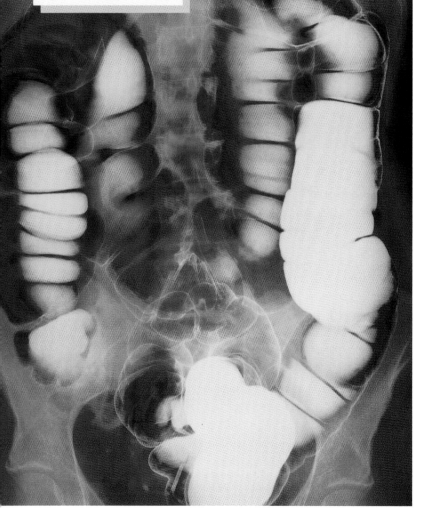

The large intestine

The large intestine gets its name because it is wider than the small intestine, but it is actually much shorter. It consists of the colon, the rectum, and the anus. A mushy paste of waste food moves very slowly through the colon.

Undigested food

Undigested food consists of **fiber,** the hard parts of fruit, vegetables, and grains that the digestive juices cannot break down. It is mixed with digestive juices, water, **bacteria,** dead **cells** from the lining of the intestines, and **mucus.** Leftover bile gives feces a brown color. The more fiber the paste contains, the easier it is for the colon to move it through.

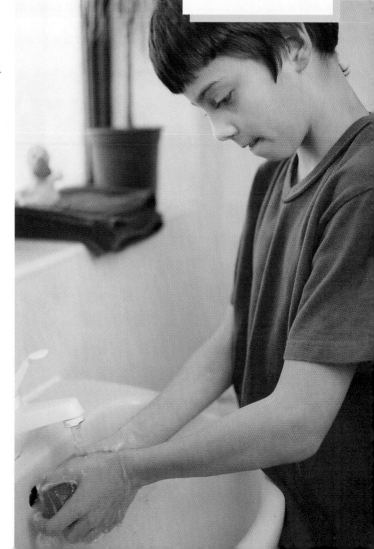

Bacteria that live in the large intestine can make you sick if they get into your stomach. It is important to wash your hands after going to the bathroom.

Water

Water with minerals dissolved in it moves through the walls of the colon into the blood. Not all the water is absorbed, however. About three-quarters of feces is water. It helps the feces pass smoothly out of the body.

Bacteria

Bacteria in the large intestine make certain vitamins that the body needs. They pass through the intestine walls and are absorbed into the blood. These bacteria also produce the gases that make feces smell bad.

WHY DOES MY STOMACH RUMBLE?

Your stomach rumbles when you are hungry. It is letting you know that your body needs a new supply of food.

Your stomach rumbles when it is empty. The muscles in the stomach wall contract and squeeze, but the only thing in your stomach is digestive juice. It is the sound of the digestive juice whirling in your empty stomach that makes the rumbling sound.

Feeling hungry

A rumbling stomach is a sign that you are probably hungry. You also feel hungry when the amount of sugar in your blood falls. Feeling hungry makes many people irritable, but, more important, it makes you want to eat. Your body needs a regular supply of different kinds of food.

Why we eat food

Food gives us the nutrients—parts of food that the body uses—that our bodies need to survive. Most food is turned by the body into energy. Every living **cell** in the body needs energy to do its job. Other nutrients make new cells. Most cells last only a few days or a few months. Dead cells have to be replaced and children need to make millions of extra cells as they grow. Food also provides many of the special chemicals your body needs to stay healthy.

Everything you do uses energy that your body gets from food. Food gives you all the nutrients you need to be healthy.

Different kinds of food

The three main kinds of nutrients are carbohydrates, fats, and proteins. Carbohydrates and fats give you energy. Proteins give you energy too, but, more important, they help to make new cells. Fat also helps to keep you warm. In addition, the body needs small quantities of important chemicals—**vitamins** and **minerals.** Many foods contain a mixture of nutrients. Cheese, for example, contains protein, fat, and several vitamins.

If you chew a mouthful of bread for a long time, it begins to taste sweet. The enzymes in your saliva have changed some of the molecules of starch in the bread into sugar.

Carbohydrates

Carbohydrates include sugar and starches. Potatoes, rice, and anything made with flour, such as bread and pasta, are rich in starch. During digestion, **enzymes** break down the starch into simple sugars. Carbohydrates are the first foods to be digested.

Digesting carbohydrates

Enzymes in your saliva start to break down starch into sugar. Enzymes in the stomach carry on the work and some sugar is absorbed into your blood through the walls of the stomach. Sweet things such as fruit, sweet drinks, and chocolate contain sugar that is quickly absorbed through the stomach. Starches take longer to digest and give you a longer-lasting supply of energy. Most starch is digested and absorbed in the small **intestine.**

Proteins

Fish, cheese, milk, meat, eggs, and soybeans are all rich in proteins.

Other kinds of beans, lentils, nuts, and flour also contain some protein. Proteins begin to be broken down in the stomach, but they are mostly digested in the small intestine.

Fats

Fats are among the last foods to be digested. Bile from the gall bladder breaks large globs of fat into tiny drops. Enzymes then break the drops into the smaller **molecules** of fatty acids and glycerol. These are mainly absorbed in the ileum, the last part of the small intestine.

This tennis player is eating a banana to keep his energy level up. Starch is a better source of energy than pure sugar. Sugar gives a quick rush of energy that leaves you feeling more tired afterward.

ENERGY FROM FOOD

Energy is measured in calories. Ten-year-old children need about 2,000 calories per day.

Portion of baked beans	170 cal
Small bag of chips	154 cal
Portion of cornflakes	110 cal
Small can of tuna	105 cal
Boiled egg	90 cal
Slice of bread	about 60 cal
1 teaspoon of sugar	15 cal

DO I REALLY NEED TO EAT GREEN VEGETABLES?

Green vegetables contain **vitamins, minerals,** and plenty of **fiber,** all of which your body needs to stay healthy. You can get these things from other foods, such as fish and cheese, but vegetables—particularly raw green vegetables—are a rich source for these nutrients. Provided you eat a wide range of foods, you should get all the minerals and vitamins you need.

Vegetables such as these are rich in vitamins, minerals, and fiber.

Vitamins

Vitamins are special chemicals that your body needs to work properly. They are mainly known by letters of the alphabet. If you do not get enough of any vitamin, your body will suffer. If you do not get enough Vitamin C, your gums may begin to bleed. The body makes some vitamins itself. Vitamin K is made by **bacteria** in the large **intestine.**

Minerals

Minerals include the chemicals calcium, iron, potassium, and sodium. The body uses calcium to build strong bones and teeth. Iron is needed to manufacture red blood **cells.** If your body is low in iron, you will become **anemic.** Potassium and sodium are also needed for healthy blood.

FOOD RICH IN VITAMINS AND MINERALS:

vitamin A	milk, leafy green vegetables, eggs
vitamin B	fish, whole grain cereals, yeast, vegetables
vitamin C	fresh fruit, vegetables, potatoes
vitamin D	eggs, oily fish, margarine
vitamin E	olive oil, vegetable oil
vitamin K	leafy green vegetables
calcium	milk, cheese, green vegetables
iron	meat, bread, vegetables
potassium	fish, meat, fruit, vegetables
sodium	most foods, table salt

Fiber

Fiber is found in vegetables, fruit, wheat bread, and pasta. The stalks of vegetables, for example, are rich in fiber. Fiber adds extra bulk to the mushy paste that becomes **feces,** and it makes the large intestine work better. If your diet does not contain enough fiber, you are likely to become **constipated.**

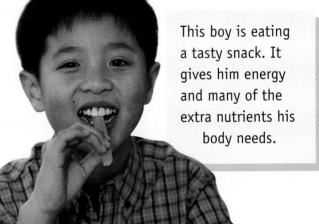

This boy is eating a tasty snack. It gives him energy and many of the extra nutrients his body needs.

WHY DO I GET THIRSTY?

The best way to quench your thirst is to drink a glass of water, but every kind of drink consists mainly of water.

You get thirsty when your body becomes short of water. The body loses up to 6 pints (3 liters) of water every day, through sweating, in urine and **feces,** and in your breath when you breathe out. Adults should drink about 5 pints (2.5 liters) of liquid a day to replace the water that is lost.

Made of water

About two-thirds of your body weight is water. Apart from body fluids such as blood, saliva, tears, **mucus,** and urine, every other part of your body, including the muscles, bones, and skin, also contains water. Even before you feel thirsty, you may get a headache and find it difficult to concentrate when your body becomes short of water. You feel thirsty when the lack of water makes your mouth and throat dry.

Water balance

All the liquids you drink contain water, and so does much of the food you eat. It is absorbed into the blood mainly through the walls of the large **intestine.** As the blood passes through the kidneys, they filter out urea—waste poison made in the liver—and any extra water and salts. In this way, the kidneys clean the blood and control the amount of water in the body. Urine is water with urea and salts dissolved in it. It is stored in the bladder until you urinate.

The kidneys filter the blood and remove extra water with urea and extra salt dissolved in it. It trickles down into the bladder, where it is stored as urine.

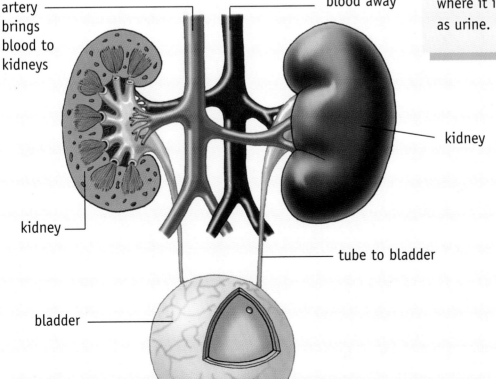

artery brings blood to kidneys

vein takes filtered blood away

kidney

kidney

tube to bladder

bladder

27

IS EATING FAT BAD FOR ME?

Fat itself is not bad for you, provided you do not eat too much. Your digestive system breaks fat down into fatty acids, which the body needs to grow new **cells,** and glycerol. The problem is that too much fat makes you fat, because any extra is stored as fat under the skin. The food pyramid shows which foods you should be eating the most to stay healthy.

Use the food pyramid to plan your meals and make sure you are eating a healthy, balanced diet.

Eating for good health

The foods you should eat most of are shown at the base of the pyramid, and the foods you should eat the least of are shown at the top. The foods at the bottom of the pyramid are carbohydrates that are rich in starch. Eating them will give you a good supply of energy. The next layer of the pyramid contains fruit and vegetables, and the layer above it contains foods that are rich in protein. The top layer contains fats and sugar. You should only eat a small amount of these.

BODY MAP

The digestive system

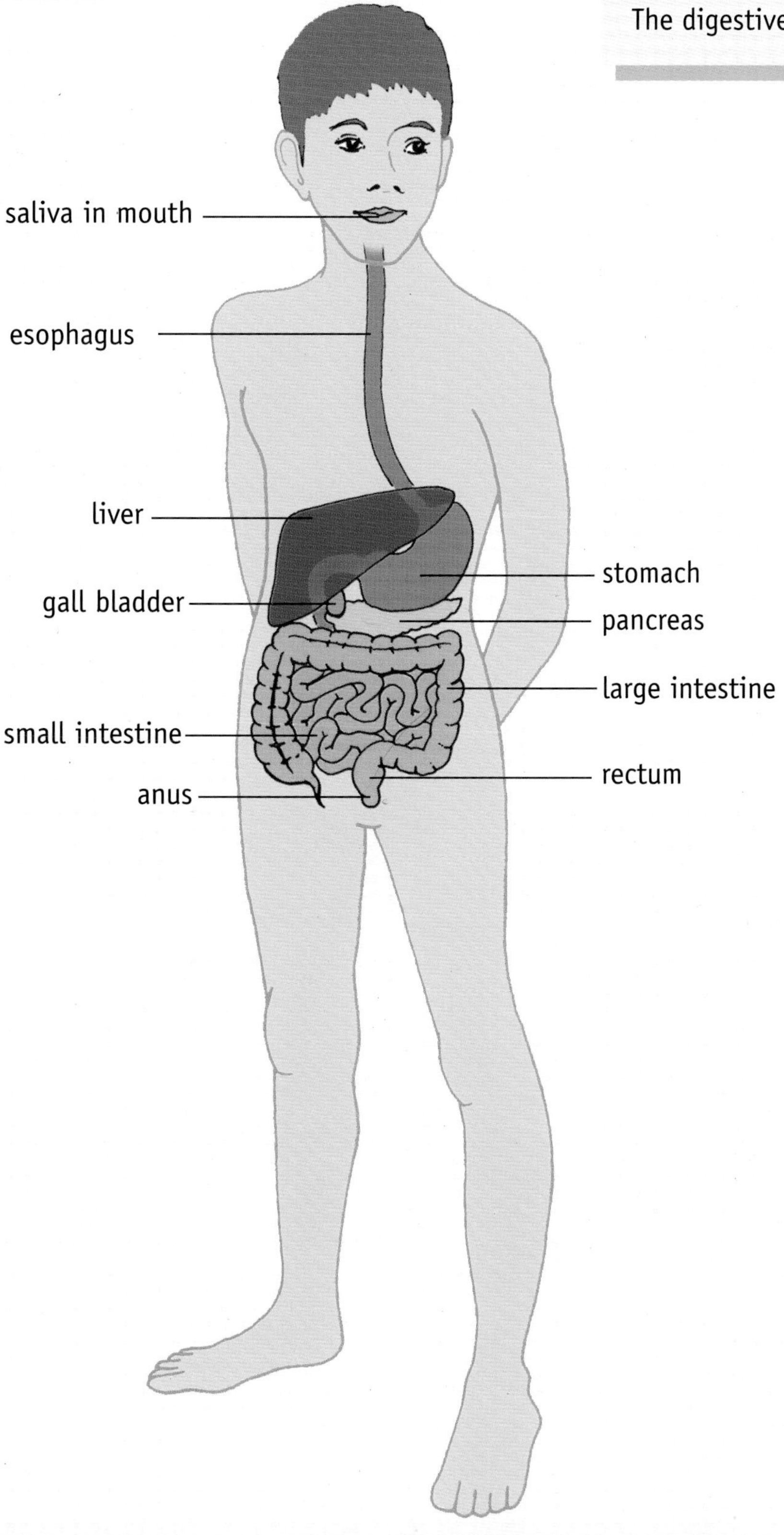
saliva in mouth
esophagus
liver
gall bladder
small intestine
anus
stomach
pancreas
large intestine
rectum

GLOSSARY

anemic having an illness that makes you feel weak and tired. It is caused by a lack of iron in the blood.

bacteria tiny living things. Some kinds of bacteria are germs that cause disease.

cell smallest building block of living things. The body has many kinds of cells, including skin cells, blood cells and cells that make the intestines.

constipated when the feces are too dry to pass easily out of the body

diaphragm sheet of muscle between the lungs and the belly

enzymes special chemicals that break down food so that it can be digested

esophagus tube that joins the throat to the stomach

feces solid waste that leaves the body when you go to the bathroom

fiber hard parts of fruit, vegetables, and grains that the body cannot break down

gastric to do with the stomach

glands parts of the body that produce particular substances such as sweat and saliva

intestine long tube that food passes into after it leaves the stomach

mineral chemical found in rocks and soil. The body needs several minerals that it gets from the food you eat.

molecule smallest particle that makes up a substance

mucus slimy liquid produced by the lining of the nose, bronchial tubes, and other parts of the body

valve device that allows liquid or gas to flow in one direction only

vitamins chemicals found in food that your body needs to stay healthy

FURTHER READING

Patten, Barbara. *Digestion: Food at Work*. Vero Beach, Fla.: Rourke Publishing, 1996.

Royston, Angela. *Eating and Digestion*. Chicago: Heinemann Library, 1997.

Stille, Darlene. *The Digestive System*. Danbury, Conn.: Children's Press, 1997.

INDEX